CONSUMER GUIDE®

10 Best Investments
from $1,000
to $5,000

Authors: David Marcum, Robert H. Meier, and James B. Powell
CONSUMER GUIDE® Investment Series Consultant:
Gene Mackevich

Contents

CONTENTS

Introduction

During the 1950s and 1960s, the average person didn't need a financial background to make intelligent investments. Many people saved a part of their income on a regular basis. They bought houses that usually increased in value over time and represented their largest single investment. Occasionally, they invested in stock in a blue-chip company such as IBM or U.S. Steel. Some investors were rewarded when they bought the stock of a young company that had no history of success but looked promising. Years of steady accumulation, through saving and patience, usually paid off in a comfortable, if not extravagant, lifestyle or retirement.

The 1970s taught us that when it comes to investing money, the familiar, simple ways don't work anymore. Most of us are not rich enough to hire professional money managers and we face some formidable threats. For example, inflation became a monster in the late 1970s. It eroded retirement savings and lessened the value of earnings. Prices for everything from gasoline to chicken to shoes increased at an alarming rate. During the same period, interest rates soared in an attempt to brake inflation. In the late 1970s and early 1980s, interest rates rose to levels previously considered illegal in most states. Laws had to be rewritten so that the federal government, credit card companies, and other lenders couldn't be prosecuted for being in the "loan shark" business. This "boom and bust cycle" of the American economy, which started in the early 1970s, is still with us today. In addition to this economic upheaval, the federal government also moved in the early 1980s to deregulate the entire industry that brings various investment opportunities. Not only is the economy harder to understand, the role of investment institutions has blurred. Banks no longer offer merely savings accounts and Certificates of Deposit. They sell bonds and manage stock portfolios. Traditional brokers now offer a myriad of products and services. Deregulation has generated an explosion of new financial products and investment opportunities.

Within the last few years, for example, new financial products such as options on currencies, indexes, and stocks have been developed. Some exchanges are linked so that futures and/or option contracts can be traded for much of the 24-hour day. New issues of stocks from high technology companies are flooding the market. New companies are going public with increased frequency, adding to the increasing number of stock investment possibilities. A wave of buy-outs and mergers have further complicated the picture. Let's face it, there are many new products, some confusing new jargon, and a lot of new rules for making money. A lot of investor confusion and lack of direction has resulted from all this activity.

The purpose of this book is to help you understand some new financial strategies and some investment instruments that may be unfamiliar. We will analyze ten investments that take advantage of new investment options. An explanation of each investment, against the backdrop of our assumptions concerning the future of the economy, also will help you understand why they have been recommended.

Understanding current investment opportunities and taking advantage of them is not as difficult as it may seem. Apart from learning about some of the new investment options and the best times to buy and sell them, you need to create realistic investment and portfolio goals for yourself, selecting investments that are fundamentally and psychologically appropriate — those that are comfortable for you. Probably, not all of the ten best investments for $1,000 to $5,000 will be right for you. Some may be too tame for your taste, while others may seem a bit risky. Still others may interest you because you enjoy the topic or concept of the investment. Even though they range over a wide spectrum, these investments all have the following important characteristics in common:

• They can be acquired through a traditional broker or specialty salesman.

• Most have been around for a few years and have historically shown that good profits realistically can be made under the right conditions by the average person. None of them are too "tricky" for the average person to understand.

• Although they all are inherently riskier than a bank account insured by the Federal Deposit Insurance Corporation, many of them carry no more risk than more familiar stock and bond investments. Each of the ten recommendations carries a different degree of risk, which is discussed clearly.

• All ten investments are fairly liquid — you can buy and sell them with relative ease. Hard-to-sell investments are not included in this book.

• They all can be purchased for as little as $1,000 and sometimes less. Within the range of $1,000 to $5,000, it is possible that substantial profits will be reaped on each investment. None of the investments need more than a $5,000 commitment to make them profitable.

- They don't need any more money than initially invested and all need to be monitored regularly, but not minute by minute.

- All ten investments have a tradition behind them, as well as regulatory laws, which helps protect the investor from fraud. It must be pointed out, however, that investors can and have been defrauded in *every* investment area. Prudent, cautious action and thought must be taken before money is invested in these, or any other investment.

INVESTING YOUR MONEY WISELY

Before choosing a specific investment, there are general rules that should be followed. These rules often make the difference between success and failure, no matter the investment chosen.

- How rich do you want to be? Generally, the richer you want to be, the more risks you have to take. Are you a risk taker or are you a conservative investor? Are you somewhere in between? Many people wish to become extremely rich and yet invest their money very conservatively. These two concepts usually are mutually exclusive. If you have no intention of risking loss, you had better stick to U.S. government securities and money market funds.

INTRODUCTION

- Despite your dreams of wealth, it is always wise to keep much of your investment capital in a very safe instrument, such as a bank CD or money market fund. The percentage of your total funds invested should decrease as the risk increases. The importance of this rule often is a function of age. Younger investors with more earning potential can risk more than those close to retirement.

- The financial risk of an investment is often closely linked to the amount of knowledge you have about the investment, which is why it's important to understand the background of an investment. For example, if the U.S. stock market is booming in March and early April, many novices may jump on the bandwagon in the middle of April because they presume a trend is developing. More knowledgeable investors may believe the infusion of IRA money, which will essentially be cut off on April 15, is driving the market. They will wait until after tax time to see if the bull stock market is fundamentally strong and not a result of a "ripple" of buying from a single source of money.

- If you make a profit, put at least half of the profit into your "safe" funds. Do not put it all back into another investment with the same or higher risk factor. You would be surprised at the number of people who have made big money by choosing the right investment, but end up losing their profit by plunging all of it back into an investment that was equally risky, or riskier, than the one that made them all that money.

- If you are in a losing investment situation that doesn't appear to give any hard evidence of a near-term turnaround, accept your loss and get out. This rule perhaps is the single most important difference between successful and unsuccessful investors. Pride and ego play no part in making money. The best investors always say "I was wrong" without hesitation — and they say it before they lose too much money. Generally, you can lose money easier than you can make it.

CHOOSING AND COMMUNICATING WITH A BROKER

Careful selection of a broker and the need to work with him or her on a professional basis is as important as choosing the specific investment. A broker can be an extremely valuable ally in the quest to make money, but do not overestimate the limits of a broker's ability or his proper role in your investment planning. The ultimate responsibility for your investment rests with you and not your broker. Lawsuits, disappointments, and misunderstandings can result from miscommunication between clients and brokers.

A broker is much like a waiter in a restaurant. He can tell you what is on the investment menu, highlight which items are popular with clients, and give you the outlook for a particular investment based on his company's in-house research, much the way a waiter gives personal comments on the foods he has tasted that day. Expect competence from your broker, and look for one who inspires your trust and confidence.

What a broker can't do is make your decisions for you. Brokers make their money when you buy and sell investments, not when you chat about the Russian wheat crop or whether the Bears will win the next Super Bowl. Therefore, they are valuable to your investment plan, but that value is very defined. They should not be making your investment decisions.

The most important thing to remember about communicating with a broker is to keep the relationship professional. Questions should be to the point and pertain to your particular investment goals and ambitions. When you place an order, make it official, not just an informal comment. Make sure your broker repeats your instructions and contacts you when your order is filled. Written confirmation from the brokerage firm always follows the verbal order and confirmation. Above all, keep accurate, clear, and concise records of all your transactions.

Economic Overview

Before specific investment recommendations can be made, a reasonable, balanced outlook of the economy for the next three or four years is needed. How the economy performs as a whole, over long periods of time, ultimately affects all investments. For example, if interest rates rise sharply and stay at high levels, housing sales will probably tend to slow over time, property will drop in price, and a recession may well be at hand. Alternatively, if the economy is strong and inflation is moderate, the volume of real estate purchases will likely be high and be accompanied by rising prices. Obviously, either scenario would heavily influence your decision to buy real estate.

When you choose an investment, even a bank CD, you are predicting that your money will multiply, because you believe the investment will move in a specific direction and with a specific safety factor regarding the original capital investment. One cannot be 100 percent sure of the direction of the impending move, however; it is always a matter of probability.

All investments are affected over time by the general direction of the major forces of the economy, such as tax policy, inflation, interest rates, oil prices, consumer spending, producer prices, the banking system, and other factors. Investments also are affected by intermediate and short-term factors. These factors may temporarily reverse or halt the general direction of a particular investment. Such situations can be dangerous to the beginning or novice investor, but if they are anticipated, they can be profitable. They are dangerous to the novice because he can be easily misled into believing a *fundamental* change in direction has occurred. He may bail out of an investment too soon, or at a loss — a loss that could have been averted through patience. Patient investors can profit in the short term from these temporary reversals, but even if they are ignored, they should continue on their long-term, profitable track.

While these temporary reversals or halts to the profitable flow of an investment may seem like a crisis, they can also be opportunities for adding to a fundamentally solid position. The Chinese understand this concept. Their symbol for crisis has two components: danger and opportunity.

Intermediate factors, such as a drop in inflation or steel production, cannot be anticipated as easily as the broad sweep of economic direction, but if investments are monitored properly, these intermediate factors often can be seen in advance and adjustments made, if necessary.

For the most part, short-term factors such as the economic impact of a terrorist attack, a Russian nuclear disaster, or the sudden downturn of a foreign stock market are not reliable or useful indicators for the average investor. The effect of these short-term factors can last from only a few hours to a few days, too brief a time for most people to profitably act upon them.

If you are right about the general direction of the economy and you regularly monitor your investments, you will undoubtedly make money more often than lose it. That is the essence of making money through investments.

THE DIRECTION OF THE U.S. ECONOMY

Our assumptions concerning the direction of the U.S. economy are reasonable, given recent economic performance. Of course, major events that conflict with these assumptions could dramatically change this overview. In that case, some of the recommended investments would not be nearly as good as we predict under the present outlook. Following each investment recommendation are types of events that most threaten the profitability of that particular investment. If those happen, you can get out with your profit intact, or with a minimal loss. Monitoring your investments against the backdrop of ever-changing economic, political, and social situations is mandatory if you are to do well. As long as the basic movement of the economy follows our assumptions, all these listed investments should do well indeed.

The recession that began in 1980 and ended in 1983-84 is well behind us. The growth that the economy has experienced in 1984, 1985, and 1986 will moderate, but positive growth in the economy will continue. Beyond 1986, we anticipate some significant changes. These changes will probably occur slowly, but the U.S. economy can be extremely volatile, so being watchful is important.

The following assumptions concern the major components of the U.S. economy through the end of the 1980s. The assumptions and opinions expressed below are exclusively those of the authors, and lay the foundation for the specific investment recommendations that follow.

• **Gross national product (GNP).** The economy will continue growing, but real growth will be less impressive toward the end of the decade. While reported growth in GNP may increase rapidly over the next four years, real growth will be less because of increasing inflation. A recession is not likely before late 1988 or 1989.

- **Inflation.** The continuing weakness of the dollar against major currencies and the increasing cost of foreign products will raise inflation to much higher levels than in 1985. The late 1980s may well see inflation at double-digit levels, much the same as 1978-79. Higher federal deficits also radically increase the probability of much higher inflation in the years ahead.

- **Interest rates.** Interest rates, on balance, probably bottomed out in late 1986. Generally, interest rates will likely be above 8 to 10 percent for the rest of the 1980s. As inflation increases, interest rates will also move higher.

- **Government spending/deficits.** While product price inflation, union demands, increasing oil prices, and a politically nervous world were much to blame for the rate of inflation in the late 1970s, much of the impetus for increases in the Consumer Price Index (CPI) will come from increasing government deficit spending in the late 1980s. Government spending and deficits may well be the major economic problems of the late 1980s; their combined impact is higher inflation.

- **Spending and industry growth.** Consumer spending will continue to increase as the economy grows. Traditional smokestack industries, such as steel, are likely to make a comeback as the dollar continues to weaken against foreign currencies and as high-tech retooling in the 1980s affects those industries. Housing will continue to grow in the late 1980s, but not as fast as before. By that time, a majority of the baby-boomers will be homeowners. Service and high-tech industries will blossom. Domestic cars will continue to be moderate to strong in sales if they maintain quality levels comparable to those of foreign competitors.

- **Banking.** The impact of Third World debt on U.S. banking will become more critical and dangerous. U.S. banking failures will increase. This will cause a crisis of confidence in all western banking systems and perhaps Japan.

On balance, we see a continually improving and growing economy through the end of the 1980s. The picture, however, is clouded with the possibility of higher deficits, higher interest rates, and inflation — with an accompanying increase in the CPI. A bank crisis before 1990 is almost unavoidable. The possibility of another inflationary spiral around 1988 or 1989 is moderately high.

THIS BOOK'S METHOD FOR EVALUATING THE INVESTMENTS

Each investment is analyzed in the areas that follow:

- **Type of investment area.** The category of the investment is defined. For example, the investment may be a stock, bond, insurance, or real estate.

- **Explanation of how the investment works.** The economic mechanism that drives the investment is discussed. An understanding of the investment's mechanism is very important, particularly with new financial products.

- **Time frame of investment.** Some investments must be bought and sold within a particular period of time. Others have no time limit; therefore, you must rely on the market indicators to tell you when to sell. Because each investment is analyzed, knowing when to get out of your investment will not be a mystery.

- **Risk/reward level.** Some investments are inherently riskier than others. Using a relative scale of one to ten, each investment is analyzed for risk. It is imperative to know the risk level before you invest your money.

- **The level of attention needed.** Some investments invariably move slowly or the changes in them affect investors slowly. Therefore, they can be reviewed every few weeks or months. Others, by their very nature, need to be monitored weekly or daily. Each investment is rated as to the amount of attention needed.

ECONOMIC OVERVIEW

- **The amount of expertise needed.** Some investments need more specialized knowledge or expertise than others. Although the following investments were chosen for their relatively low complexity, these investments do differ. Each is ranked for the amount of expertise required.

- **Caveats and pitfalls.** These are events or scenarios that could undermine the value of your investment.

Within this structure, the analysis of each investment should help you decide which investments are suited to your needs, goals, aptitude, and interest.

Evaluating the Recommended Investments

Each of the following investments has been selected for either maximum potential returns given its risk factor and liquidity, or its ability to generate returns with little monitoring.

Some of you may like all ten investments, others may feel comfortable with as few as three or four. In any case, to protect your portfolio, it is wise to diversify your investments to limit your risks. Remember, risk is a relative term. The risk ratings assigned are not scientific, but they do give you a perspective on where the risk of these investments fits in comparison to other investments.

To visualize what these risk ratings mean, keep in mind the following generalizations:

EVALUATING THE INVESTMENTS

Risk level is indicated by numbers one through ten. Each investment is assigned a range to signify the low to high risk of that particular investment, given the future economic picture outlined in the previous section.

Number one (1) represents a fully insured Federal Deposit Insurance Corporation (FDIC) bank Certificate of Deposit held at a highly solvent bank. This is as close to risk-free as possible.

Numbers two (2), three (3), and four (4) represent relatively low-risk investments, such as blue-chip stocks.

Five (5) can be visualized by the example of a relatively well known, but smaller company stock; in other words, a moderate risk.

Numbers six (6) and seven (7) get progressively more risky, that is, the original capital invested is exposed to higher risk of loss.

Eight (8) is a risky investment, where the capital investment is exposed to a high risk of loss.

Number nine (9) is pure speculation.

Number ten (10) represents investing a large amount of money in an expedition to find buried treasure indicated on an old pirate's map. In other words, very high risk.

Please note: The order in which these investments appear have no bearing on the strength of the recommendation. Each investment has its own strengths and weaknesses, which are clearly stated.

Mutual Funds

RISK LEVEL: 5–6

One of the recent favorites of the average investor has been mutual funds. Mutual funds are all organized in a similar fashion, although some differences appear among them. In principal, they all function in the following way:

A management company hires professional money managers in the area of fund specialization. Shares or units of the fund are sold by the management company for a specific amount per unit or share. These shares usually cost between $500 and $5,000 each. The money received, minus any sales commission and/or yearly administration fee (if applicable), is pooled by the management company. The money managers then trade and invest the pool of money as they see fit, within prospectus guidelines, given their research and expertise. The unitholders or shareholders (you, the public, or financial institutions) usually receive dividends or payouts on a regular basis. These payouts are based on the profits made by the fund. Usually, a performance fee of 10 to 15 percent of the gross profit is paid off the top to the money managers. It is an incentive plan. The more money they make for you, the more they make for themselves.

To most people, mutual funds usually imply "stock mutual funds." It is true that mutual funds often specialize in one or two investments, but there are many different types of mutual funds specializing in different instruments or securities, including money markets, U.S. blue-chip stocks, foreign stocks, high-tech stocks, bonds, tax-exempt bonds, precious metals, and literally dozens of others.

In some cases, large brokerage or investment firms will sponsor their own mutual fund or group of mutual funds. Usually, these groups will contain a common stock, money market, and federal government bond fund. Sometimes, as investment dollars grow, specialty funds will develop in certain areas, such as aggressive growth stocks, high-technology stock, and tax-exempt bonds.

One of the key developments that came out of the creation of groups or "families" of funds is the ability to switch your money from one fund to another via the telephone. In other words, if you had your money in a bond fund at a brokerage company, you could call the broker and have him switch the money to the common stock fund with little or no charge, if you believed it would become a better investment than the bond fund. This "telephone switching" has become very popular in recent years and the technique has even spawned at least one highly successful newsletter, which concentrates on just this feature of mutual fund investing.

The technique of switching from one managed fund to another also has become popular in the new variable life insurance programs. In some of these, your equity in the life insurance can be shifted (up to four times a year, at your discretion) to one of several different professionally managed mutual funds within the insurance program.

Being able to move your money at will from one professionally managed fund to another is definitely an advantage over being stuck in one investment or having to set up new accounts every time you want to get into a new investment. Although this mutual fund scenario sounds dynamic, exciting, and like a potential bonanza for every investor, there are a couple of major problems. First, not every investor understands the economy like a professional money manager. This makes wise decisions concerning where and when to switch money very difficult. A wrong switch at the wrong time can cost you in money and in lost opportunities. Second, within a specific group of funds, there may not be a good balance of types of investments to allow the investor's money to work to great advantage all the time. Let's face it, just trying to understand where the economy is going is hard enough. Knowing which particular mutual funds, at a given time, will be the best for your financial goals is even harder.

An alternative to switching is a new breed of mutual fund that has recently been introduced to the market. Instead of investing in only one type of instrument, (e.g., common stocks or tax-exempt bonds), the mutual fund acts as an umbrella company which controls several different "sub-funds." Each sub-fund operates independently of the other sections and each sub-fund money manager is totally responsible for the perfor-mance of his sub-fund. If a specific sub-fund money manager doesn't perform as well as should be expected, he or she can be fired and replaced.

This replacement would be done by what is known as the allocation strategist. He or she monitors all the sub-funds and consults with the various specialty money managers on a regular basis. More importantly, the allocation strategist des-ignates what portion of the fund's money goes into each sub-fund. The parameters that dictate the percentage that goes into each sub-fund depend on the direction of the economy, what is performing well, and what is losing value. The key factor for the average or novice investor is that the "switching" is not done by the shareholder. It is done by a professional or group of professionals for the investor. Certainly, the overall performance of the fund relies on the performance of the money managers and the allocation strategist, but in cases where top quality people are filling the positions, they invariably will do much better than an amateur investor.

Looking at the overall performance of various market categories, we see tremendous differences between 1976 and 1985. The fact that we have seen, just in this time period, inflation between 4 and 20 percent, recession and strong recovery, prime rates between 9 and 21 percent, oil between $5 and $36 per barrel, and the Dow between 700 and 1800 shows that just one mutual fund cannot optimally perform to your best advantage over long periods of time.

The really important question, as it pertains to successful investing in mutual funds, is this: Can the average investor anticipate the amount of increase and timing of the different yields from these four (or other combinations of) investments as shown in the following table? Probably not. This means that mutual funds that can automatically switch internally from one sub-fund to another may likely be the mutual funds of tomorrow. An asterisk (*) denotes the winner each year of the four choices.

COMPARATIVE YIELD OF INVESTMENT

Year	U.S. Stocks	Foreign Stocks	Precious Metals	Bonds
1976	+23.6%*	+3.7%	−4.1%	+15.6%
1977	−7.4%	+19.4%	+22.6%*	+3.0%
1978	+6.5%	+34.2%	+37.0%*	+1.2%
1979	+18.5%	+6.2%	+126.5%*	+2.3%
1980	+32.5%*	+24.4%	+15.2%	+3.1%
1981	−5.0%	−0.7%	−32.8%	+7.3%*
1982	+21.6%	−0.7%	+15.3%	+31.1%*
1983	+22.5%	+24.8%*	−16.3%	+8.0%
1984	+6.2%	+8.1%	−19.2%	+15.0%*
1985	+31.7%	+56.8%*	+5.8%	+21.4%

Source: CDA Investment Technologies, Inc. U.S. stocks measured by Standard & Poor's 500. Foreign stocks measured by EAFE Index (Europe, Australia, and Far East), denominated in U.S. dollars. Precious metals measured by London daily gold price. U.S. fixed income bonds measured by Shearson-Lehman Government/Corporate Bond Index. Past performance of each of the categories should not be interpreted as indicative of future performance.

Look at the results. Over a ten-year period, the U.S. stock market was the big winner twice. Foreign stock markets rated the best twice.

MUTUAL FUNDS

Precious metals had the highest increases for three years, and U.S. bonds did the best three out of ten years. The four investments had a pretty even balance over the time span. What's more impressive is that if you had placed the majority of your money in the winners each year, the yearly percentages are wonderful: 23.6 percent; 22.6 percent; 37 percent; 126.5 percent; 32.5 percent; 7.3 percent; 31.1 percent; 24.8 percent; 15.0 percent; and 56.8 percent! Of course nobody would put all of their money in one of these "baskets," but professionals could at least tell where the likely places for the best increases would be.

RECOMMENDED MUTUAL FUNDS

There are not a great number of these "umbrella" funds available. One of the most highly recommended is the **Blanchard Strategic Growth Fund.** The Blanchard Strategic Growth Fund makes itself even more unusual in the world of mutual funds by allowing the allocation strategist to move money from fund to fund, but only within certain guidelines, as laid out by the prospectus. These guidelines are:

U.S. stocks. Minimum 10 percent of total fund assets and a maximum of 50 percent.

Foreign securities (stocks). Minimum of 10 percent of total fund assets and a maximum of 50 percent.

Precious metals. Minimum of 10 percent of total fund assets and a maximum of 50 percent.

Fixed income securities (bonds). Minimum of 5 percent of total fund assets and a maximum of 70 percent.

Before investing in any mutual fund, make sure you read the prospectus and, if possible, find a fund that diversifies as much as possible.

The Blanchard Strategic Growth Fund is at 150 E. 58th Street, 36th floor, New York, NY 10022; 212/750-0555 or 800/922-7771.

Other more traditional growth mutual funds have shown good to excellent returns during the past couple of years. Three to consider are:

Fidelity Magellan Fund, Attn: Account Information, 82 Devonshire Street, Boston, MA 02109; 800/225-6190.

Lindner Dividend Fund, Inc., Attn: Account Information, P.O. Box 11208, St. Louis, MO 63105; 314/727-5305. (Currently closed to new investors, but a reopening or a spinoff fund are possibilities.)

Nicholas Fund, Inc., Attn: Account Information, 700 N. Water Street, Milwaukee, WI 53202; 414/272-6133.

INVESTMENT RECAP

Type of investment. The Blanchard Strategic Growth Fund, a type of mutual fund.

Time frame of investment. You can leave your money in for whatever amount of time you wish, from just a few weeks or months, up to several years.

Risk/reward level. This investment is rated at a 5–6. Mutual funds can be risky, although the public will undoubtedly have forgotten that fact in light of the tremendous bull market in stocks seen over the last couple of years. Almost every stock mutual fund made all-time high profits. In a down market, however, specialty stock mutual funds in particular can do very poorly. The Blanchard Fund should score very low on risk, because of the diversity of the fund's investments. It is rated a 5–6 at this time, because of its short track record.

Level of attention needed. This type of investment doesn't really need much attention. The purpose of its structure is to be a literally "carefree," one-stop investment vehicle. Because the company is young, however, make sure you watch the overall quality of its performance at least monthly and compare it to the performance of other similar mutual funds.

Amount of expertise needed. Again, virtually none, but read the prospectus carefully so you

have a basic understanding of how the fund works
and what affects the value of the four investment
categories.

Caveats and pitfalls. The major danger for this
investment is if the allocation strategist mis-
judges the economy and allocates money to the
wrong area. The returns may not be what they
could have been. Fortunately, the money can be
shifted rapidly, but lack of track record is still
the main consideration here. Ultimately, everything else being equal, the actual chance of losing
a great deal of money should be less than with a
"one investment focus" mutual fund.

Municipal Bond Funds

RISK LEVEL: 4–5

Tax-exempt or municipal bonds are a popular type of investment. They encompass a greater number of types of tax-free government issues than those issued by municipalities and cities. To the public, they are important for three reasons:

- The interest that tax-exempt bonds earn from the government issuer may be free from both federal income tax and state income tax in the state they are issued. For example, if you are in a 30 percent tax bracket and your tax-exempt bonds earn 10 percent interest, it would be as if you were earning an annual, taxable income of almost 15 percent. Not too many relatively secure investments give that kind of a return.

- With top-rated (AAA type) bonds, the possibility of a major loss in the value of the investment is small. The payment of interest is often guaranteed by insurance in AAA bonds. For all intents and purposes, the faith and backing of the issuing form of government (state, county, city, etc.) literally guarantees their repayment.

- Municipal bonds are usually liquid. Tax-exempt bonds of high quality, whether bought and sold singly or by a tax-exempt mutual fund, are one of the easiest investments to acquire or sell.

Many investors have turned to mutual funds to invest in municipal bonds. These bond funds have become popular, because the minimum investment is low. Actual tax-exempt bonds may cost thousands of dollars — far beyond the financial means of most investors. Investments in mutual funds often require as little as $500.

The financial services industry generally offers two different kinds of funds. One type is conservative, buying only top-rated (AAA or AA), insured bonds. The other buys much lower rated bonds; this gives higher returns but at greater risk. Many different bonds are bought by each fund, so that even if a handful defaulted on interest payments, the overall loss would be inconsequential as a percentage of the fund and the loss is absorbed by profits on other bonds.

When you add up these advantages, tax-exempt bonds sound like one of the best investments available. In fact, they can be desirable, but they do have one flaw. As debt instruments, their face value is particularly vulnerable to rising interest rates. In fact, wildly escalating interest rates can obliterate the value of shares in a bond fund in no time.

BONDS AND RISING INTEREST RATES: JUST LIKE OIL AND WATER

All bond funds are vulnerable to the effects of rising interest rates. The following example explains how this works.

Let's assume that the city of Chicago issues a new $1,000 tax-exempt bond at 8 percent interest. The bond matures in ten years. If you purchased the bond and everything remained static in the marketplace, you would receive 8 percent or $80 per year for the life of the bond. When the bond matured, your principal would be returned.

Let's assume that after only one month, the Chicago bond issue is trading in the market. Interest rates move up to 10 percent and Milwaukee issues a new $1,000 tax-exempt bond that pays the new market rate of 10 percent. If a new bond is trading at 10 percent, then the 8 percent rate (represented as $80 per year) being paid on the Chicago bond is not very interesting to investors. If you wished to sell your bond in this environment, you could never sell the bond for $1,000. Why should somebody pay you $1,000 to get an 8 percent yield when they could pay $1,000 and get 10 percent?

You would have to sell the bond at a price that turned the annual $80 payments into a real 10 percent return. To do that, the bond would sell for $800 — a loss of $200 (20 percent of $1,000) in the value of the bond. On a $1,000 bond, an interest rate rise of one interest point translates into a loss of 10 percent on your investment. Likewise, if interest rates move down, a bond's value will increase. When interest rates rise, bond prices move down. When interest rates decline, bond prices rise.

At the end of the 1970s or early 1980s, when interest rates climbed to 20 percent and more, the bond market was a wholesale slaughterhouse and portfolio values collapsed like a house of cards. Of course, if a fund is trading bonds, it can sidestep some of the downward pressure caused by increasing interest rates by selling and buying the profitable issues. You, as a fund investor, however, are still not totally immune from the possible negative effects of increasing interest rates.

MAKING INVESTORS' MONEY SAFER

In the 1950s and 1960s, interest rate fluctuations were minor compared to the gyrations we have experienced in the last few years. There were very few ways to "hedge" a position in bonds and the concept of hedging was generally ignored. Now, interest rate futures contracts and interest rate options on futures can be used to protect a bond position or portfolio from a fall in value. The number of ways that you can protect bonds from a rise in interest rates are many. One is shorting a Treasury bill contract on the International Monetary Market (IMM).

Shorting or selling in a commodities market (where T bills are traded) means you are betting that the value of the security is going down. T bills fall when interest rates go up; therefore, a T bill short is a bet that interest rates are going to go up. If you are correct in this assumption, the T bill short will make more and more money as interest rates move up, thereby offsetting some, or most, of the loss that the face value of the bonds is taking. The whole idea works beautifully. The only problem is that the average investor doesn't want to short T bills to hedge, for example, a $3,000 investment in tax-exempt bonds. It is simply too dangerous and too difficult to track.

So, despite the good aspects of a tax-exempt bond, average investors are up against both the problems of the value of the bond plummeting in a rising interest rate situation and in trying to hedge a position. The only reasonably intelligent way of doing this is through buying tax-exempt bonds in a fund that has an ongoing hedge program that will give some stability.

One recent introduction that takes these problems into consideration is the **Colonial Tax-Exempt Insured Fund.** This fund invests only in AAA, tax-exempt bonds that are backed by bond insurers' guarantee of the timely payment of the interest. Colonial operates the Insured Fund with a hedged position, so that if interest rates were to move up, some of the loss taken by the bonds is gained in the hedge position. An account in the Colonial Tax-Exempt Insured Fund can be opened with as little as $250, but you can invest any amount over that. Other advantages include monthly dividend payment by check, instant liquidity, and check-writing privileges. Colonial was founded in 1931 and currently has nearly $5 billion in assets under management. The Insured Fund was started in 1985. The Colonial Tax-Exempt Insured Fund's address is Colonial Investment Services, Inc., 75 Federal Street, Boston, MA 02110; 800/426-3750.

Other recommended tax-exempt bond funds are: **Seligman Tax-Exempt Fund Series, Inc.,** Seligman Marketing, Inc., Attn: Account Information, One Bankers Trust Plaza, New York, NY 10006, 800/221-2450. Seligman not only has a tax-exempt fund that invests in bonds from all over the U.S., it also has specialty tax-exempt funds that invest in specific state's bonds such as California, New York, Louisiana, etc.

MUNICIPAL BOND FUNDS

National Securities Tax Exempt Bonds, Inc., National Securities & Research Corporation, Attn: Account Information, 605 Third Avenue, New York, NY 10158; 800/661-3000.

INVESTMENT RECAP

Type of investment. Tax-exempt bonds and tax-exempt bond funds.

Time frame of investment. Most tax-exempt bonds mature over a long period of time, years or decades. Tax-exempt bond funds allow the investor to determine the time frame of the investment. Most funds allow check-writing privileges so you can close out your account immediately.

Risk/reward level. 4–5 for funds, a bit riskier for individual tax-exempt bonds. The value of tax-exempt bonds is very dependent on the direction of interest rate movements. Our outlook for the economy suggests higher interest rates in the future. This possibility is your biggest single risk with a fund investment.

Level of attention needed. Simply watch the interest rates on a weekly basis. If rates go up, the value of the bonds will fall.

Amount of expertise needed. For funds you need very little expertise. Trading is done professionally for you; however, you should watch interest rates carefully. If they are going up, you may wish to move your money into a money market fund or some investment that benefits from higher interest rates.

Caveats and pitfalls. Make sure you invest in funds or fund families that have a long track record and a history of profits. The latter exposes your investment to less risk than putting it into a small, untried tax-exempt bond fund. The greatest danger is investing directly into one bond. Some smaller cities and communities may offer tax-exempt bonds for $5,000 and under. Unless you are an expert in bonds, the fund concept is less risky.

Convertible Bond Funds

RISK LEVEL: 3–4

Convertible bonds have shown, year after year, that they offer some of the best yields on Wall Street. They are very liquid and have been around for decades. With all of the assured interest income and legal protection of a bond, they also possess the wonderful ability to change into the stock of a company whenever the stock becomes a better investment than the bond. Convertible bonds can give the investor the best of both traditional investment worlds.

The major drawback is that of all paper investments, convertible bonds are usually the most difficult for the average investor to analyze for investment potential. Successful analysis of this investment requires it be analyzed simultaneously as both bond and stock. This can be confusing.

While offering a basic guide to what convertible bonds are and how they work, this section does not delve into the complexities and dynamics of convertible bonds. They take extra effort, but they can be quite profitable. In addition to buying individual convertible bonds just as you do other securities, investments can be made in professionally managed convertible bond funds. But, like all investments, you should understand the basics and the risks before you hand over your money.

WHAT IS A CONVERTIBLE BOND?

Bonds are debt instruments. When you buy a bond from a company, you are giving the company a loan. In return for the loan, the bond pays a specific amount of interest per year. A convertible bond is a hybrid security that is originally issued just like a regular bond. Convertible bonds usually pay slightly less interest than regular bonds issued at the time. The amount you pay for each bond may vary from the face value. The price of each convertible bond depends on market interest rates, interest paid by other bonds in the market, and the outlook for bonds in general.

What separates convertible bonds from regular bonds is that in most cases, they can be turned in at any time and converted into a prespecified number of shares of common stock in the company that issued the bond. Whether or not the bond gets traded in for the stock depends on the value of the underlying stock. Knowing when it is profitable to convert is important.

There are approximately two thousand convertible securities worldwide and about six hundred in the U.S. There are other kinds of convertibles (not necessarily bonds), such as convertible preferred stock, Euroconvertibles, and foreign exchange listed (convertibles available in Japan, London, etc.). All of these are specialized markets, sometimes appropriate for the individual investor, but often more heavily traded by convertible bond funds and professional investors.

HOW DO CONVERTIBLE BONDS WORK?

There are five important parts of an initially offered convertible bond. They are, the *face value* (par), *maturity time,* the *interest rate of the bond,* the *conversion ratio* (predesignated number of shares of common stock each bond will convert into), and the *price of the underlying stock.*

Let's assume that PQR company offers a new convertible bond. It has an 8 percent coupon rate (interest paid on the bond), a $1,000 par value, matures in 25 years, and has a conversion ratio of 50. The conversion privilege remains in effect for the life of the bond. All of this information is designated in the prospectus.

With this information, the investment value of the bond can be estimated. The investment value is the estimated price as if there were no conversion feature — as if the convertible bond were a regular bond. In this case, the investment value is $1,000 so long as interest rates are also 8 percent. If interest rates drop below 8 percent, then the value of the bond would be higher than $1,000. If rates go above 8 percent, the value would be lower than $1,000.

If a $1,000 bond is paying 8 percent and a new $1,000 bond is offered that pays 10 percent, the old bond adjusts its price in the market so that it is also paying 10 percent instead of 8 percent to a new buyer. The price of the bond has to drop below $1,000. In this case it would drop to $800, so that the 8 percent represents 10 percent of the value of the bond. Likewise, if rates drop to 6 percent, then for the $1,000 bond to reflect that 6 percent rate, the price has to increase above $1,000. When interest rates fall, bond prices rise. When rates rise, bond prices fall. In other words, the bond's price will change so that its value reflects the current level of interest rates.

Most convertible bonds carry an interest rate that is lower than straight bonds. Therefore, the market will often value the convertible at lower than face value, which is reflected in its price.

CONVERTIBLE BOND FUNDS

This is to the advantage of the company issuing convertibles. They pay less interest on the bond, in exchange for the possibility of converting it into stock.

In our example, the PQR bond's conversion ratio is 50. That is, the holder of a $1,000 face value convertible bond will receive 50 shares if he converts. That means that each share has to be worth at least $20 (50 × $20 = $1,000) to make the conversion from bond to stock worthwhile. Often the conversion ratio is 20 to 30 percent higher than the stock's price when the convertible bond is issued. If the price of the stock is lower than $20, the holder will keep the bond and earn interest. After all, nobody wants to spend $1,000 for a bond and convert it into, for example, 50 shares that are worth $15 each, or $750.

Knowing the conversion ratio is not enough. Any bond can trade at a premium over its conversion value. The premium can be as low as virtually nothing, or as high as a considerable percentage. This premium over conversion value can be calculated (see the following example).

Remember, when the value derived from this formula is low, the price of the convertible bond will move more in line with the underlying stock. If the derived value is high, the bond will not move with the underlying stock. Buying convertible bonds with low premiums over conversion values usually is the most profitable investment.

Normally, a 10 to 15 percent premium is considered acceptable.

Let's assume the market price of PQR bonds is $1,075 and the value of 50 shares of stock is $20 (50 × $20 = $1,000). The premium over conversion value is calculated in the following manner:

$$\frac{\text{Bond Market Price minus Face Value of the Bond}}{\text{Face Value of the Bond}} = \text{Premium Over Conversion Value}$$

or,

$$\frac{\$1,075 \text{ minus } \$1,000}{\$1,000} = 7.5 \text{ percent}$$

Another important diagnostic tool is the premium over investment value. In this case, when the derived value is low, the price of the convertible will not drop easily if the underlying stock price collapses. If PQR stock's investment value is $900 and the market price of the bond is $1,075, the premium over investment value is calculated in the following manner:

CONVERTIBLE BOND FUNDS

$$\frac{\text{Bond Market Price minus Investment Value}}{\text{Investment Value}} = \text{Premium Over Investment Value}$$

or,

$$\frac{\$1,075 \text{ minus } \$900}{\$900} = 19.4 \text{ percent}$$

Again, you are looking for a number on the low end so that the risk-limiting aspect of the convertible is prominent.

If the stock doesn't rise in price, or temporarily looks unattractive, then the bond pays you a return on your investment. Buying a convertible bond is like buying a call option on a specific number of stocks at a specific price, except your premium pays you interest over the long life of the bond instead of disappearing when the option expires. Convertibles can be very good investments and will always provide some return on your money — so long as the company remains relatively solvent and profitable. If you convert and the stock rises in price, big gains can be made, without the outright and obvious risk of buying the stock in the first place.

Choosing the winners yourself can be very tricky, although by using these diagnostic tools, you can select well-priced convertibles, buy them, and when the value of the underlying stock becomes greater than the bond's value, you can convert.

RECOMMENDED CONVERTIBLE BOND FUNDS

Few brokers are knowledgeable in convertible bonds, but usually most large brokerage firms will have one or two brokers who specialize in the investment and can help you with this investment.

Another alternative is to invest in a mutual fund that specializes in convertible bonds. One convertible bond fund is the **Noddings-Calamos Convertible Income Fund,** Attn: Account Information, 2001 Spring Road, Oak Brook, IL 60521; 800/251-2411; in Illinois, 800/821-6458.

Other recommended convertible funds are:

AIM Convertible Yield Securities, Inc., AIM Advisors, Inc., Attn: Account Information, Eleven Greenway Plaza, Suite 1919, Houston, TX 77046; 713/626-1919.

Value Line Convertible Fund, Value Line Securities, Inc., Attn: Account Information, 711 Third Avenue, New York, NY 10017; 800/243-2729.

INVESTMENT RECAP

Type of investment. Convertible bonds and convertible bond funds.

Time frame of investment. From a few days or weeks (long enough to make the conversion and sell the stock) to the life of the bond.

Risk/reward level. 3–4 for funds, primarily because of the guaranteed interest income. Investing in individual convertible bonds can be much riskier, depending on your expertise.

Level of attention needed. If you have your money in a professionally managed fund, a monthly inspection of the fund's progress is required. If you are buying individual convertibles, weekly, if not daily, attention is needed to protect and maximize your investment.

Amount of expertise needed. Buying and selling individual convertible securities requires a large degree of expertise. To invest in a mutual fund that invests in convertible bonds, you will want to compare long-term returns of individual funds and review the prospectus of any fund you are considering.

Caveats and pitfalls. Companies can go bankrupt, although the bond gives you legal leverage in recovering some or all of your investment. If you are buying individual securities, you will want to select the bonds of larger, more secure companies. Your expectations that the underlying stock will rise may not happen. You may be stuck with an 8 percent return for years, if you don't resell the bond. Once you convert, the stock may plummet in value and you could lose much of your investment. You cannot convert the stock back into bonds if that happens.

The Platinum Noble

RISK LEVEL: 6–7

Just the word "platinum" evokes the feeling of royalty, luxury, and wealth. We have platinum credit cards, platinum editions, platinum albums, and platinum jewelry. Every time the word is used, it signifies the best.

Investing in platinum is entirely different than owning it. Most people don't know its uses (other than jewelry) and why its price changes. Therefore, they have a difficult time analyzing the quality and appropriateness of a platinum investment. Some may be tempted to buy, but they remember with fear that precious metal prices can be volatile. Others may believe they can invest in platinum only through futures trading, a very risky proposition.

In fact, platinum can be purchased in the form of one-ounce coins called *nobles,* just as gold can be purchased in the form of one-ounce coins called Maple Leafs and Krugerrands. Futures trading is not necessary. Platinum in the form of jewelry is not a good investment. Jewelry comprises only a part of the global demand for platinum, and a good percentage of the price of platinum jewelry reflects the high labor cost. The largest use for platinum in the United States is in manufacturing and industry. After a long bear market, platinum prices are finally poised for an upward move that could easily last for two to four years.

WHAT IS PLATINUM AND HOW IS IT USED?

Platinum is just one of a group of elements that are related both chemically and physically. Known as the Platinum Group Metals (PGMs), they include platinum, palladium, ruthenium, iridium, osmium, and rhodium. They are rare. Ten tons of ore are required to make one pure ounce of platinum; the metal's total production is miniscule compared to gold or silver. While world gold output is about 1,200 tons per year, platinum output is only 80 tons — approximately 7 percent of total gold production —

Platinum has some superb properties. It has a very high melting point, 1.5 times as high as gold. It is very resistant to acids, doesn't tarnish, doesn't contract or expand, is ductile, malleable, and conducts electricity beautifully. Perhaps its most important characteristic is that it is an incredible catalyst. A catalyst speeds up certain types of chemical reactions without essentially being altered in the process. Platinum is one of the best, if not the best, catalyst in the world. Its catalytic properties, fortunately, just happen to work with some of the most important industrial and manufacturing chemical reactions in modern business.

For these reasons, platinum (unlike gold) is valued more as an industrial metal than as money. Gold's primary value is as a hedge against inflation, war, and other crises, despite the fact that it is used in a wide variety of products from electronics to the nozzles of a space shuttle. Gold prices can be influenced by surprise bank failures or crop failures. Platinum, while somewhat affected by a political and economic crisis, is more powerfully affected by changes in supply and demand in the industrial sector over the long haul.

Statistically, the largest user of platinum is the Japanese jewelry trade. Lower oil prices and a stronger yen will help platinum jewelry sales. While crude oil has dropped dramatically, the price for platinum has remained about the same in Japan. Another large user of platinum is the U.S. automobile industry, which uses the metal as a key component of catalytic converters; each one contains approximately one-half ounce of platinum. Another big user is the oil industry. Platinum is used to help "crack oil" into its component parts, such as gasoline. Its use in electronics, textile manufacturing, and hundreds of other critical chemical reactions makes it an absolute necessity for seven of every ten manufacturing processes in the U.S.

WHY INVEST IN PLATINUM NOW?

Since the last bull market in platinum, which ended in early 1980, several fundamental reasons have developed which make physical platinum in the form of nobles (coins) truly attractive.

There are only three significant producers of platinum: Canada, the U.S.S.R., and South Africa. Canada alone, although the third-largest producer, could not supply all of America's platinum needs, let alone the rest of the free world. South Africa, the world's largest producer, is constantly threatened by internal strife. The U.S.S.R. is a net seller of platinum only if all their internal needs are met first. Russian policy in the event of a platinum source shutdown in South Africa is unknown. The U.S. has only one platinum source, but it still has years to go before development.

There are several reasons why platinum is a good investment now:

THE PLATINUM NOBLE

- Although the South African mines operated at capacity for most of 1985, they barely met the world's demand. Increasing global economic activity will strain the mines' capacities further.

- Bad South African political news helps the price of platinum. Platinum investments through South African mining stocks (Impala, Rustenburg, and Lydenburg ADRs) are questionable if the mines are shut down due to political turmoil. Physical platinum would skyrocket on such news. Politically, South African mining stocks are vulnerable.

- Platinum should rise in price even though gold or silver drops. If gold should move up because of international unrest, platinum will benefit indirectly.

- A recent platinum miners' strike in South Africa sent prices up. As the political situation there deteriorates further, strikes may become more common.

- Platinum demand is up. Even with South African producers working full steam, they just barely meet demand. Future demand will dig into above-ground reserves.

- Platinum hoarding and hedging by individual investors has become a small but growing force in the demand quotient. The minting of platinum nobles, wafers, and ingots has, for the first time, made platinum investing easy. In the first year of issue, more than 100,000 nobles were sold.

- Perhaps the strongest single positive sign for increasing prices, other than major turmoil in South Africa, is the large number of European countries that will require catalytic converters in all new cars. They will phase in the requirement over a ten-year period. Ultimately, demand for platinum on an annual basis could leap by 25 percent. Other countries such as Austria, Switzerland, Sweden, Australia, and South Korea are currently adopting U.S. catalytic converter standards. Certainly in the near future, demand created by these new laws will immediately boost global consumption by at least 100,000 ounces.

- Other industrial needs are being developed. New platinum-tipped spark plugs, platinum fuel cells, cancer killing pharmaceuticals, and platinum catalysts in the fiber optics industry all will add to the demand as the high-tech revolution continues.

INVESTING IN PLATINUM

In addition to physical ownership, investments can be made through South African and Canadian mining stocks. There are several reasons to avoid this move. The South African mining stocks are vulnerable. If the mines were closed, the stocks could become worthless and the price of the metal itself would soar because the only other major producer is the U.S.S.R. In Canada, platinum is usually obtained as a byproduct of mining for other products. Hence, investing in Canadian mining stocks is very complex and is not recommended for the average investor.

Platinum futures contracts can be traded in New York, but they are extremely volatile and the average investor will very likely lose his shirt when trying to beat the professional traders.

Ingots and wafers, unlike coins, are not trusted and accepted.

WHY PLATINUM NOBLES?

Platinum nobles are one-ounce coins. They have a Viking ship depicted on one side and a profile of Queen Elizabeth II on the other. They are an official coin of the British Isles. They weigh 1.000 troy ounce or 31.103 grams. Fineness minimum is 99.95 percent. They sell for just a few percentage points (usually 3 to 7) above the platinum bullion price and can be sold back to dealers at the platinum bullion price. The bid-ask spread is similar to popular one-ounce gold coins such as Maple Leafs and Krugerrands. Therefore, their value closely tracks the free market price of platinum.

Platinum nobles are liquid. Current prices can be conveniently checked weekly, unless metal prices are extremely volatile. They then should be monitored daily. Stay away from buying sub-ounce nobles (they are available), because the smaller the size, the more the sales commissions take as a percentage of the price of the coin. If you cannot buy all the coins you want at once, buy them over time, at regular intervals. By the time you accumulate what you want, the average price per coin you pay will not be high — considering where the price can go in the future. Platinum cost more than $1,000 per ounce in 1980.

Nobles are sold by many coin dealers, brokers, and banks that deal in precious metals.

INVESTMENT RECAP

Type of investment. Platinum noble coins.

Time frame of investment. There are many theories about the pricing cycles of the precious metals, including platinum. Some analysts seem to think that gold and platinum run in about six-year cycles. Others make no claims on these cycles. Ultimately, the market price should indicate when to sell. Nobles can be sold at any time to coin dealers, brokers, and banks that trade precious metals. Currently, platinum appears to be low in price, although it has already made some significant gains since its early 1980s lows. Assume that this investment will take twelve to thirty-six months, but be prepared for the price to soar sooner or for the price increase you are waiting for to come later. The historical price of platinum gives this investment growth potential.

Risk/reward level. Platinum is a precious metal, which makes its price vulnerable to many different political, economic, and technological factors. The risk is higher than some other traditional investments, simply because the price is so volatile. This volatility makes the risk potentially higher and some investors find this nerve-wracking. The price may in fact collapse by 50 percent or more under certain circumstances, although platinum, by its very nature, always has some amount of value. Given the fact that at one time the price was more than $1,000 gives precedence to the concept that it may go up that high again.

Level of attention needed. On a weekly basis, check the metal's value (Friday's closing price) and interest rates. If rates go up, platinum prices may fall. If platinum prices fall and you own some nobles, you may want to sell them; if you don't own any nobles, you may want to keep an eye on platinum prices for a while before buying.

Amount of expertise needed. It would help to talk to a broker and possibly learn more about platinum and the other precious metals if they are unfamiliar to you. Keeping track of prices on at least a weekly basis is mandatory.

Caveats and pitfalls. If you work with a reputable, longtime precious metals broker, you will pay, within a couple of percentage points, what any other broker will charge for nobles. Buying at a good price is not the issue with nobles. The main pitfall to investing in nobles is keeping track of prices and not getting too greedy. If platinum moves up sharply after you buy the coins, take a profit. Don't wait until you can "get the most." Invariably, the people who wait too long miss the profit altogether. Also, platinum is very volatile. Prices can jump up and down in the short term. Don't get panicky at the first sign of a drop in price; it may only be a technical correction in the market before the price soars.

Industrial Automation Stocks

RISK LEVEL: 6–7

Before the turn of the century, the industrial revolution in America changed the life of every citizen more than all prior technological changes combined. New inventions continued to raise the standard of living of the working person to a level greater than the wealthiest people only a century before.

The change also created friction between management and workers, as demonstrated by the implementation of the automatic loom in the nineteenth century and the attacks made by textile workers on that machine.

We are in the midst of another great industrial revolution, perhaps greater than the previous one. The high-technology world is reducing the number of workers in the manufacturing sector. Although this is happening everywhere, the public is perhaps most aware of it in the steel industry. Layoffs were common in the early 1980s, and not everyone was recalled during the economic recovery. High-technology retooling dramatically reduced the number of labor hours needed to produce a particular item. American manufacturing businesses may be poor employers, but they are still very strong in manufacturing products. Approximately 30 percent of the gross national product in the U.S. each year is in manufacturing.

There is a strong reason this high-tech trend will continue. The global trade capability of the world is such that almost everything in terms of the cost of money (interest rates), raw materials, energy, and capital goods is virtually the same everywhere. The big difference is in the cost of the labor to make the product. If Americans are to keep the high hourly pay levels they have become accustomed to, they must out-produce by several times their foreign competitors who work at a considerably lower wage. The only way to do this is through factory automation.

Whether or not this "progress" is desirable is best left on the academic podium. Like it or not, industrial automation is a new, thriving industry and over the next twenty or thirty years, we will see changes that will boggle the mind. Nothing can stop this trend in America, unless we want to give up approximately 30 percent of our gross national product (GNP). Of course, if nothing else, politicians will not allow that to happen, even if it takes the most incredible tax credits imaginable to force the retooling of our factories. Already, some factories, particularly in the area of paper, plastics, and containers, have become so automated that only three or four people can run a factory that produces as many high quality products as one that employed thirty to fifty people in the past.

There are caveats. New industries are full of new companies. New companies are known to go bankrupt, and high-tech companies can go broke simply because they didn't keep up with the technology of the competition.

Another warning about this "high-tech bonanza" is to not be lured by what Wall Street calls the "sizzle." Some stocks are popular with investors because the companies' products are considered nifty or "sexy" — things like robots, lasers, cryogenics, gene splitting, and artificial intelligence. Just because they sound like Buck Rogers does not mean they will make big money now or in the future.

GETTING BACK TO BASICS: INDUSTRIAL AUTOMATION

We said earlier that we are in a new industrial revolution — a high-tech miracle that is changing the face of manufacturing. Industrial automation is basic. This is where it starts and this is where the ongoing incomes, dividends, and eventual fortunes will almost assuredly be made.

In reality, industrial automation falls into two different categories. They are:

• Factory Automation.

• Process Control Automation.

Factory automation includes areas such as robotics, computer-aided design and computer-aided manufacturing (CAD/CAM), and automated material handling.

Because millions of people in Third World countries are willing to work for low wages, robotics is a slowly growing field; robot-workers with artificial intelligence and vision are essentially too costly compared to low-paid workers.

Computer-aided manufacturing (CAM) is the ability of a factory to make a single product or part of a product, often on an assembly line basis, with little or no human involvement. This is now one of the fastest-growing areas. As man reaches into space, computer-aided manufacturing will have untold applications in the future.

Computer-aided design (CAD) has received much publicity and will grow well in the years to come. The problems encountered in such diverse areas as marketing/packaging and complex aerodynamic structural details will be solved more easily by CAD.

Automated material handling simply is what it implies. Handling of materials, parts, and finished products are handled by computer-controlled systems. Men are no longer needed to carry, lift, stack, and push items around a factory.

Process control automation (PCA), the other aspect of industrial automation, is an area that most people know little about because it essentially lacks "sizzle." It is dull and boring, but PCA is the automation of the creation, processing, handling, and packaging, all in one smooth operation, of a single product. PCA is used extensively in chemical, plastics, and paper mill manufacturing. Its applications are immense, and it will spawn industries that will make megabucks.

BUYING THE WINNERS

If you ask the typical broker about industrial automation stocks, he will probably mention robots and tell you it is a bad investment. Wall Street perceived high-tech stocks as a good investment a few years ago, gave them lots of press, brought investors in to the circus, and the stocks fell flat on their faces in the recession of the early 1980s. Wall Street was not wrong to highlight these stocks, but they were too early in their vision and didn't remind investors that this is a long-term investment. New industries don't become profitable overnight, no matter how widespread the revolution. Plan to hold the following recommended stocks for four to six years.

RECOMMENDED INDUSTRIAL AUTOMATION STOCKS

A CAD/CAM company:

Computervision (Code CVN; NYSE). A pioneer company with proven products for many applications. New interests include semiconductor design. The company tripped up in 1985 by not keeping up technologically with its main competitor, Intergraph. Although Intergraph is the largest company currently in the CAD/CAM area, more profit will likely be made as Computervision comes back, which it is now doing.

Automated manufacturing companies:

Cross & Trecker (Code CTCO; OTC). This automated machine tool firm is capable of producing total, factory-wide industrial automation systems. It is so successful that the Japanese use it as their model for factory automation. To survive, the heavy, basic industries in the U.S. simply must have a company like Cross & Trecker, which has not yet begun to realize its potential.

Cincinnati Milacron (Code CMZ; NYSE). The largest machine tool manufacturer in the U.S., it also supplies industrial robots and plastic-processing equipment. It does smaller automation jobs than Cross & Trecker, but it is well known and used by small- to medium-sized manufacturing companies.

A process control automation company:

Accuray (Code ACRA; OTC). This supplier of process control systems specializes in servicing the paper, sheet metal, plastics, tobacco, and timber industries. The company enjoys prosperity in both European and American markets. Its products are excellent, have high quality, and are in constant demand.

INVESTMENT RECAP

Type of investment. Industrial automation stocks.

Time frame of investment. The concept of this investment can actually last for many years, perhaps decades. Industrial automation is an area that will gradually develop, continually expand applications, and eventually be used in high-tech manufacturing in outer space. Specifically, however, these stocks should do nicely as the economy continues to grow, smokestack industries continue to retool, and as America moves more toward a high-tech, service-oriented society. A comfortable time frame for these stocks to "mature" is about four to six years. If the economy grows strongly over the next decade, some of these types of stocks may become the "blue chips" of the 21st century.

Risk/reward level. We have rated the risk level of this investment at a 6–7. As stocks, these have the tremendous potential of a growing industry. They also have the danger of dropping in value because they may fall out of the investors' favor, or another company may develop in this youthful industry and surpass the recommended stocks with a new idea. Compared to the current blue-chip issues, these stocks will be more volatile.

Level of attention needed. On a monthly basis, compare the value of the U.S. dollar to other major currencies, such as the Japanese yen and German deutsche mark. If the dollar is strong, the U.S. won't be competitive with the rest of the world, and retooling of our factories may slow down, thereby lowering the value of these stocks. Also pay attention to the general state of the U.S. economy. If a recession occurs, these stocks may fall.

Amount of expertise needed. Although you don't have to understand how a factory is automated, it is a good idea to know which companies utilize automation technology and how they relate to one another in performance, experience, and profitability. Full service brokerage houses usually do regular research on stocks in this field.

Caveats and pitfalls. Prices for these types of high-tech stocks can move up and down rapidly. There are two main pitfalls in making industrial automation stock investments. The first is that the volatility of the stock price may scare you and panic you into selling at a loss, when in reality you should be holding on to the stock for the long term. The second pitfall is that new companies, particularly in the high-tech field, can fall on hard times just because they miss a technological turning point. Another company could race by the one you hold in a matter of months. Careful monitoring of the stock's price and of this sector's economic news will help protect your investment. Don't be complacent about this investment.

Single Premium
Life Insurance

RISK LEVEL: 3–4

Even the best whole life insurance policies offered
during the 1950s and 1960s were terrible investments; a basic bank savings passbook could often
beat their returns. The insurance industry,
however, has gone through a major revolution
during the last decade or so, discarding old types
of policies and providing alternatives to attract
insurance buyers who demand returns that are
at least equal to other conservative and/or traditional investments. While still reluctantly providing basic term insurance at relatively inexpensive
rates, today's insurance companies focus on
offering customers both high returns and death
benefits.

SINGLE PREMIUM LIFE INSURANCE

Life insurance used to be justified as a form of forced savings, albeit with a very low return. With automatic deposits and withdrawals now readily available, consumers can easily save as much as the insurance premium payments and get a better return than the old life insurance policies ever allowed. The insurance companies have caught up with the times. They now compete relatively well against other financial services and products.

COMPETITION BREEDS CONFUSION

The proliferation of new insurance products is confusing. First, there was term and whole life. Term insurance is inexpensive, and it doesn't create a savings account for the owner of the policy. It only pays off when the owner dies, and if the premiums are paid up to date. For many, it still is a very good form of insurance, especially if you want to protect your family with a large amount of money in case of your untimely death.

Whole life used to resemble a combined "savings account" and term insurance. The longer you paid in, the more "cash value" (the amount you could receive if you cashed in or cancelled the policy) you earned. Of course, no matter when you died, the death benefit (face amount) was there. Often, the policy owner would die before the cash value was greater than the face amount because rates of return were quite low.

Whole life insurance lost its attractiveness in the 1970s, when the paltry, predetermined interest rate that was paid was destroyed by high inflation. The industry's answer to this dilemma was the universal life and the variable life insurance policies. Universal life allows for flexible premiums with current rates of return, and no market risk. The cash value grows at an interest rate usually guaranteed for 90 days to one year.

The variable life insurance policy has developed over the years into the following concept:

The amount of money you pay into the policy is placed into one or more mutual funds. These mutual funds manage and invest the money on the behalf of the insurance company that, in turn, manages and invests the money on behalf of the policyholders. The insurance company may dictate which fund or funds the money goes into, or you, the policyholder, may decide. If the money is placed into successful mutual funds, your insurance premium payments can earn much higher rates than they ever could in a bank or similar investment. Of course, the rates vary depending on many factors. Some months you may do well, others may not be so good. On balance, though, a professionally managed fund will outperform a savings passbook, often by a wide margin.

Because of the relatively high interest and/or dividend payments that some of these variable policies offer, the cash value of these policies can actually move higher than the face amount of the death benefit well within the policyholder's lifetime. Because of this, the insurance company will allow you to cash out your policy at any time, even if the cash value is more than the death benefit. If you die, the highest figure, either the death benefit or the cash value, will be paid to your heirs or estate.

This type of life insurance is usually offered with annual, semiannual, or monthly payments. Often the payments will stretch out two or more decades before the insurance company finally allows you to stop paying and labels the policy as "fully paid-up insurance."

ENTER SINGLE PREMIUM LIFE INSURANCE

For some, the concept of single premium life insurance makes a lot of sense. This type of life insurance is self-explanatory. Instead of paying for life insurance for twenty or more years, you make a single payment up front. No other payments are ever needed! No matter what happens to your job, savings, or investment portfolio, you never have to pay another cent to maintain your fully paid-up insurance.

Of course, if you get any quantity of life insurance coverage, the single premium is going to be hefty.

SINGLE PREMIUM LIFE INSURANCE

A few start as low as $3,000. Many are $5,000 and some go even higher. So what are the advantages and disadvantages of making this kind of investment?

Single premium life insurance puts a fully paid life insurance policy into your hands. No matter what happens in the future, your heirs will be taken care of. Also, you can buy fully paid-up insurance on your child for a single premium that is low compared to the amount of coverage given. And the growing cash value makes the purchase a nice investment for the child.

Unlike life insurance where you pay in over many years, single premium life gives you a high amount of cash value immediately and this builds over the years. In a standard, single premium whole life, the returns are predesignated. In the more popular single premium variable life, the returns vary according to the investment success of the mutual funds which manage the premium payments. If they are successful, the cash value of the policy can be appreciably more than the regular type of variable life.

Finally, the amount of insurance you can buy with a single premium is much greater than what you can buy on the long-term payment plan. In other words, the amount of premium needed to buy whatever amount of life insurance you want is considerably less with single premium life. For example, a regular, variable whole life policy with

SINGLE PREMIUM LIFE INSURANCE

a face amount of $25,000 may cost you $600 per year from some companies and will not be paid up for twenty years. It costs $12,000 to buy $25,000 worth of death benefits (granted, this is strung out over the long term). Some companies may charge $5,000 for the same paid-up coverage on a single premium variable or whole life policy.

There are, however, some problems with this approach. Although you can buy a lot of face value insurance for your money while you are young, the face value of the policy drops regularly for the same single premium payment as you grow older. For example, while a 20-year-old could get $25,000 worth of coverage for, say, $5,000, a person over 40 might get only half of that coverage for $5,000.

Another problem is the rate of return paid by the mutual funds. If they are well managed, this can be a good long-term investment. If they are not well managed, you may be disappointed. Often, the insurance company will allow you to switch your policy to one which has a guaranteed, flat rate of return within a certain period of time, if you are unhappy with the returns of the variable policy.

Since single premium life insurance is a relatively new product and none of the companies can boast an excellent, long-term track record, it will help you to look at the overall track record of the insurance company's mutual funds that manage regular variable life premiums. Quite possibly, they will be the same funds that handle the single premium.

Also, you will have to shop carefully. Almost every major company is now offering single premium life. Because this sort of policy is a new product, no specific recommendation can be made at this time.

INVESTMENT RECAP

Type of investment. Single premium life insurance.

Time frame of investment. A single premium life insurance investment is good for as long as you live, or until the cash value far exceeds the single premium payment. In the latter case, you may wish to "cash in" and spend it or invest the money elsewhere.

Risk/reward level. This investment is a 3–4, very conservative and quite safe. If you buy from a large, old, and established insurance company, there is almost no chance of losing your investment. At the very least, you have the cash value. More likely, however, your investment will grow at a faster rate than a bank account. The investment is not rated a 1–2 because so many of the mutual funds which will manage the premium payments have short track records. Also, the full faith and backing of a major insurance company is not as good as the faith and backing of the U.S. government given to Treasury securities.

Level of attention needed. During the first year or two, it would be wise to pay particular attention to the yield. If it is unsatisfactory, in most cases you can alter the policy to a nonvariable rate policy. After that period of time, quarterly or even yearly observation of the growing cash value of the policy is important. Under a plan in which you choose the mutual fund, careful selection, possibly with the help of a financial planner or other financial professional, will be helpful.

Amount of expertise needed. Most investments require careful monitoring after you buy. This one needs care *before* you buy. After you pay for the insurance, no real expertise is needed. The expertise you need is to carefully compare the different policies offered by the companies. Don't be pushed into signing by a high-pressure salesman.

Caveats and pitfalls. Do your homework and get outside advice if you feel confused — *before* you buy!

Oil Stocks

RISK LEVEL: 7–8

If you would have predicted in early 1985 that oil would precipitously drop from a high of $39 per barrel to below $15 per barrel by the second quarter of 1986, you would have been categorized with those who always predict the end of the world.

For more than a decade the inflationary nature of oil prices very profoundly etched certain messages in our psyche. One was that oil company stocks were long-term investments. Another was that oil stocks had only cyclical weakness; when stock prices dropped, it was because the company had either made a big financial mistake, had a major oil spill, had legal or IRS problems, or was the victim of a cyclical slowdown in consumer demand. While those assumptions operated for more than ten years, the recent crude oil price collapse has changed the game. Instead of buying and holding any company's stock that had income derived from oil, you now have to be selective and limit stock trades to companies with clean balance sheets and capable management.

It also seems that once a major commodity has advanced at will for so many years and finally crashed, the roller-coaster price ride just begins. Anticipating when to get in and out of the industry will require an unusual talent.

Currently, most analysts are neutral to negative about many oil stocks. Some oil stocks will turn around, but it will take awhile.

IN SIMPLE TERMS, WHAT IS GOING ON?

A study by Nalcosa Consulting Company of Geneva, Switzerland, has shown that at $15 per barrel, eleven of thirteen OPEC countries will continue to lose money if production is continually increased. These countries include Algeria, Gabon, Nigeria, Ecuador, Libya, Venezuela, United Arab Emirates, Iran, Iraq, Indonesia, and Qatar. Notice that Saudi Arabia is missing from this list. Remember also that Saudi Arabia alone has oil reserves for at least 200 years.

Collapsing prices are due to Saudi overproduction, coupled with less demand in the free world. The Saudis couldn't bring OPEC to an amicable agreement on oil prices. Therefore, they increased production to take a larger share of the pie and force down other OPEC oil prices. Each OPEC member is responding to Saudi Arabia by producing more oil so they will not be squeezed out entirely.

Some have speculated that this is a master plot by Saudi Arabia to drive their weaker competitors out of the market, particularly in America. The very low oil prices may ultimately bankrupt many exploration, distribution, and drilling companies here, forcing us once again to depend on Saudi oil. The Saudis deny this theory. Regardless, there remain some basic things one should know in order to profit from oil.

• Although oil investments are long-term, you cannot buy oil-related stock and sit with it until eternity. Buying and selling will become part and parcel to the oil industry stock environment.

• At this point, oil companies with low debt and/or those that wield power in the U.S. retail oil product market will be the ones to watch domestically. Non-oil-producing foreign companies that sell oil products and have low American exposure also will probably be doing well.

- Oil cannot stay at this low price forever. Already there is a "creep back" from the lows. In certain parts of the country, gasoline collapsed initially but has now recovered. The impetus for the Saudis to coordinate an effort to raise prices is strong. At the height of their power, the Saudis had a cash glut of U.S. dollars in the $160 billion range. That has since dropped to around $50 billion. They are not poor by a long shot, but this precipitous price drop has hurt them.

- As companies go bankrupt in the U.S. and abroad, competition will deteriorate, thus allowing OPEC, or the Saudis alone, to once again gain control of the oil price. When prices will start moving again, however, is anybody's guess. As mentioned earlier, oil investments are long-term. If you are in a hurry to make money, this is not the investment for you. For those more patient, a full recovery in oil, and the subsequent dividends and capital gains in selected stocks, may very well make the wait worthwhile.

RECOMMENDED OIL STOCKS

Our selections are the companies that are relatively debt-free, have an ability to buy right, and are aggressive in their retail marketing of products.

Our recommendations are:

Exxon (Code XON; NYSE). It is the world's largest integrated oil company. Its average daily sales in 1984 were approximately $2.4 million. Its U.S. reserves are estimated to be about $22 billion. Exxon has a good dividend yield of about 6.5 percent and provides tremendous safety simply because of its size. Its marketing is strong and should do well in keeping its market share from others.

Royal Dutch Petroleum (Code RD; NYSE). With a recent dividend yield of 6.7 percent, it appears that Royal Dutch saw the handwriting on the wall before others and adjusted to a lower oil price early on. It is running efficiently, cash flow is good, and it does not have a large U.S. exposure; U.S. sales are only 26 percent of total income. The fall in the dollar has helped it. The company also has a great safety factor due to its size and diversification.

Amoco (Code AN; NYSE). With an above average amount of safety, Amoco's balance sheet and projected future earnings look healthy. Good retail marketing will carry this sixth largest petroleum company through the tough times ahead, although a quick turnaround is not to be expected.

As the economy changes, other companies may come into favor, and indeed, the above list is not all-inclusive. Consulting with your broker and reading timely research analyses by the better brokerage houses may well be worth the effort, if and when you decide to invest in selected oil stocks.

INVESTMENT RECAP

Type of investment. Selected oil stocks.

Time frame of investment. This is a strictly long-term investment. Since the character of oil stocks has changed so dramatically since the big price drop in crude oil, this is an investment to buy at a low price now and sell at a higher price later. Our prediction is that this investment will take three to six years to develop, depending on the western economy, inflation levels, and the ability of OPEC members to get their act together.

Risk/reward level. This investment is rated at a higher risk level than some others, because it is questionable if OPEC can ever come to an agreement on the international price of a barrel of oil. Without OPEC cohesiveness, it is likely that oil can remain at current, or slightly higher, levels for many years to come. If oil does move up significantly in price over the next few years, the oil stocks could do quite well. Although oil could still go lower, the probability that it will go higher over time appears stronger.

Level of attention needed. You should check the price of your stock weekly. Fortunately, whenever OPEC meets to discuss pricing and production of crude oil, it is always highlighted in the news and can be easily monitored.

Amount of expertise needed. An oil investment requires very little expertise. Watching what OPEC does, having done some homework on the companies before you buy, and observing the overall trend in oil stocks will eventually tell you when to sell and make a profit. Special knowledge is not needed here.

Caveats and pitfalls. There are three major pitfalls here. First, oil may not come up in price for years to come. This will make your stock investment probably less attractive than some others. Second, you may get bored waiting for something to happen and sell just before the big increase and/or at a loss. Third, you may choose the wrong individual stock. Do your homework on the possible oil companies. Although we believe our recommendations will hold up (barring a major economic change), some fundamental facts concerning our recommended companies may quickly change. Consult current research papers on oil-related stocks before investing money.

National Real Estate Stock Fund

RISK LEVEL: 7–8

One of the most interesting of all investments is the REIT, or Real Estate Investment Trust. REITs were designed to give the average investor a convenient way of obtaining the capital appreciation and income of owning real estate without the trouble of managing the property. By the mid-1970s, REITs had gone out of control with poor management, bad investment and loan policies, and a general downtrend in economic growth. Prices collapsed. Now they're back with better management, more prudent investment and loan policies, less debt, and higher quality properties — and they are back in the middle of a growing economy. The outlook for some is good, others are so-so. The question is: How can an average investor obtain the advantages of an upward-bound real estate market in REITs without getting burned by owning the wrong one?

WHAT IS A REIT AND HOW DOES IT WORK?

REITs are relatively simple in concept. They are like a mutual fund in that they are run by professional management. They invest directly in such things as apartments, shopping centers, and housing developments. They also may invest in mortgages on office buildings and residential properties. A few may do both. Shareholders receive regular statements, either quarterly or biannually, have the right to receive dividends and capital gains distributions, and can sell their shares on a major or over-the-counter exchange.

REITs are economical for the average investor. While real estate limited partnerships may cost a minimum of $1,000 per unit, some REIT shares sell for as little as $25. REITs also do not have the problem of continual IRS scrutiny, as do limited partnerships. REITs have become very popular; 146 REITs were being offered to the public by 1985.

REITs are required by law to keep at least 75 percent of all assets in real estate and hold all investments for at least four years. This regulation helps keep the money managers away from short-term speculation, a risky and often losing proposition. Finally, the law provides that REITs distribute 95 percent or more of their income to shareholders. In other words, they cannot pyramid their positions with no return to those who risked their money.

THREE DIFFERENT KINDS OF REITS

REITs come in three distinct forms: equity, mortgage, and hybrid. Each is different enough in its investment philosophy to exhibit a tremendous variance in performance.

Mortgage REITs exclusively loan money for construction and mortgages. Equity REITs share in the value growth of tangible real estate and earn the bulk of their profits when they sell property, although they also receive income in the form of rent. Hybrids do a little of both.

In dividends, mortgage REITs beat all others in 1985. Averaging a 12.29 percent return, they beat both equity and hybrid REITs with 8.48 percent and 9.56 percent respectively. From 1984 through 1985, the share price index for all three types showed that, although dividends were high on mortgage REITs, share prices actually dropped 1.35 percent. Hybrid REITs lost 0.24 percent. Share prices for equity REITs were up 1.57

percent. Total returns on equity REITs were a whopping 18.4 percent, while average mortgage REITs actually dropped 9.93 percent. Hybrids averaged a +5.08 percent return.

Each one of these REITs also are divided into two different other groups: self-liquidating and perpetual-life. Self-liquidating REITs have a specific life span. At the end of that span, all properties, equities, mortgages, loans, and other elements of the REIT are liquidated. The total amount of return, minus any administration or performance fees, is disbursed to the shareholders. Perpetual ife REITs are open-ended, and can buy and sell property throughout their existence.

In general, REITs must be analyzed with the following points in mind:

• *Good management*. Trusts with at least five to ten years of management experience will likely show better profits.

• *Low debt/good balance sheets*. The normal debt to equity ratio is one-to-one. Highly leveraged REITs are dangerous. Whether a REIT has a good balance sheet and low debt will be made clear in the prospectus.

• *Regular dividend growth*. Apart from the big profit that can be made by selling a property, you should look for regular dividend payments that are made on time, as well as fairly regular dividend growth. Consistency in management will contribute to this regularity of payments and growth.

• *Diversification.* Not only should the portfolio range over many types of real estate (shopping centers, houses, a limited amount of offices), it should also range geographically. This is important. Texas is a recent example. The recent plunge in the price of oil ultimately will lower real estate values there. A REIT that solely concentrates, for example, on Houston or Dallas real estate will shortly be in deep trouble.

Stay away from REITs heavily invested in office buildings. Usually, the fewer investments that are made by the REIT in office buildings, the better, because this real estate sector has many pitfalls.

In general, it appears that REITs specializing in health care facilities and public shopping malls and centers are doing well. Your broker should be able to help you in these areas.

THE EGGS IN A BASKET DILEMMA, ONCE AGAIN

Despite all of these points concerning REITs, the elements of inherent risk in a single or focused area of real estate investment are intimidating.

Real estate values no longer move steadily up. They can collapse in price as well. Various types of real estate can be affected adversely by a host of different situations, from mortgage defaulters to depression in a single industry (e.g., oil).

RECOMMENDED REIT FUND AND REITS

Because average investors have only a certain amount of money that they can afford to place in a certain area, the danger of choosing the wrong REIT deters some people — and with just cause. It would be a shame, however, to let a good-to-excellent opportunity in the real estate area slip by. Our recommendation to minimize your risks is the **National Real Estate Stock Fund** in New York.

You can invest as little as $500, you have access to all or part of your investment on a daily basis, dividends are paid quarterly, monthly withdrawal programs are available, and you can switch your investment to other funds offered by this organization.

The National Real Estate Stock Fund is owned by the low-profile, but highly respected, National Securities and Research Corporation, with $1.7 billion under management. The NRESF invests in a multitude of real estate and construction-oriented investments, but regularly has between

NATIONAL REAL ESTATE STOCK FUND

30 to 40 percent of its investment in various types of REITs. While this is not a direct REIT investment, it does allow average investors to benefit greatly from well-chosen REITs without the hazard of picking their own out of a large field. The fund is not foolproof, but professional and experienced management can bend the odds in your favor.

The NRESF also invests in stocks that have promise and are, in some way, related to the building and construction trade.

Because real estate has become a tricky investment for many people and direct ownership participation is exceedingly expensive, REITs are a good potential investment, particularly with the outlook for greater inflation. Picking the winner, however, is somewhat of a shot in the dark. The recommendation of the National Real Estate Stock Fund at least partially cushions the average investor from those dangers, and offers what appears to be a professional and conservative way of investing in real estate. The NRESF may be reached at 605 Third Avenue, New York, NY 10158; 212/661-3000.

Currently, some of the best individual REITs that have performed well have a majority of their investments, either equity or mortgage, in mall-type shopping centers. Two REITs specializing in shopping centers around rapidly growing cities are **Federal Realty** and **Pennsylvania REIT.**

Federal's trading symbol is FRT and can be found on the New York Stock Exchange. Pennsylvania REIT, whose symbol is PEI, can be traded on the American Stock Exchange. Both of these REITs have good track records and appear attractive for future gains. Before you invest, read specific brokerage house and other independent research on specific REITs before you invest or send money. The detailed research and care will likely pay off in profits and better peace of mind.

INVESTMENT RECAP

Type of investment. Real Estate Investment Trusts, The National Real Estate Stock Fund.

Time frame of investment. Regular REITs should be bought and sold with the real estate price cycles. They act much like regular stocks and bonds, but follow the ups and downs of the real estate market instead of the stock market. REITs that specialize in certain geographical areas of the country may go down early or late in the cycle, depending on the particular economic situation in the area. REITs that invest nationwide will more likely follow the trend. Buying and selling should be geared to that cycle.

As with regular REITs, the performance of the National Real Estate Stock Fund will be cyclical. But because of the NRESF's diversity, its ups and downs should be less violent than with some regular REITs. Still, this fund should be purchased in an upward moving or stable real estate market and sold when prices are obviously beginning to move down from a peak. In short, either an investment in a regular REIT or in the NRESF will continue to be a good investment for at least several months and perhaps for several years, depending on the flow of the economy.

Risk/reward level. This investment is classified as a 7–8 or relatively high risk. Its value is very vulnerable to the capricious moves of interest rates, political and legislative events, tax law changes, and population shifts. Prior to the 1970s, interest rates fluctuated far less vigorously than now. Current fluctuations can turn a bust into a boom, virtually overnight, and vice versa. The risk is high but so is the potential reward in REIT investments.

Level of attention needed. An investment in the NRESF will bring you statements every quarter. Also, you can check on the value of your investment by calling the fund from time to time. Since the fund is diversified throughout the rainbow of allied real estate investments, it should be more stable than a regular REIT. Regular REITs can be volatile in price; therefore they should be followed just like stocks and bonds.

Amount of expertise needed. Like the Blanchard Strategic Growth Fund, the NRESF is designed to allow a nonexpert to take advantage of the real estate market in a diversified portfolio. The expertise needed here is in either selecting regular REITs or in judging the time to sell regular REITs or units in the NRESF fund. When interest rates are predicted to jump over a period of several months, you might want to follow the fund or REIT more carefully and even sell to capture profit. Remember, it is always better to take a small profit than to lose what you have in anticipation of a greater profit.

Caveats and pitfalls. Other than the timing and careful selecting, the recent changes in the tax law may have some bearing on REIT investments. Before investing in the NRESF or any particular REIT, take the time to talk to your accountant or tax attorney concerning the new tax laws.

Buying a Second House or Condominium

RISK LEVEL: 6–7

Buying a second house or condominium is a distinct possibility for many before they reach their golden years. The tax law changes enacted in 1986 preserved deductions of mortgage interest on second homes, making them one of the few tax-favored investments available. Through very careful shopping, planning, and some seller financing, it is possible to buy a property with less than $5,000 down. It also is possible to build equity after purchase by renting the property to a tenant, and applying the rental payments to your mortgage.

Because of the many variables of this investment, it is the least specific of the recommended investments in this book. There are five key things to consider about this investment.

• What do you want to buy? Do you want a retirement home somewhere in the South? A vacation place that you use now and eventually sell or move into later? Defining what you want to buy helps limit your options, as different financial situations require different limits. Your personal goals, as well as investment goals, also will narrow your choices.

• Tax law changes regarding depreciation and other property-owner items make it imperative to avoid a situation that could turn into a negative cash flow on your investment. It is more important than ever to be able to rent the property on a regular basis so that you can avoid future expenditures of capital. Do you want to rent it for thirty years until the time comes when you can move into a fully paid residence? Or do you want to sell at a huge profit? Do you want to rent it seasonally and vacation there yourself? Some parts of western Florida have shown this potential. You must find an area that either rents easily or offers a competent rental management company that can do the work for you.

• Your second residence must be affordable, including the mortgage payment, maintenance expenses, taxes, and utilities. If you begin with a small down payment, will the payments be reasonable enough that you will not be pushed into economic disaster in case you are without renters for a period?

• How motivated is the current owner to sell? Sellers who often are flexible about the selling price and down payment include those who are retiring, have changed jobs, been divorced, have lost a job, or whose children have "left the nest." If the owners are in good financial shape but simply want to move, the price may be flexible, and the owners may be willing to help you with the down payment.

• Although a bank sponsored mortgage is the most common way to buy property, some types of seller financing, with or without bank loans, may help to get what you want with a minimum investment. An understanding of the basics of seller financing is extremely important. The details of the process should be explained to you by competent realtors before you sign an agreement or contract. This chapter is not a substitute for professional advice.

WAYS TO BUY THAT ARE CHEAPER THAN NORMAL

Let's assume you have found a one-bedroom condominium on the west coast of Florida that the owner is selling for $49,000. No real estate company is involved. There are several ways you could buy this property after a price has been negotiated.

The most common way to finance your purchase is through a bank. Normally, the bank will require a cash down payment of 20 percent of the purchase price. What you would really like to do is to buy the condo with much less than $9,800, to avoid locking up your capital.

Two alternatives to a traditional bank loan are a Veterans Administration (VA) and a Federal Housing Administration (FHA) loan. Interest rates on these loans are frequently less than prevailing mortgage interest rates and the down payment may be considerably less than 20 percent. A realtor can help you determine if you are eligible for either loan.

Another alternative is to assume the owner's existing loan, when the interest rate is lower than what is currently offered. Paying the owner for his equity in the property may then be negotiated so that you pay a small amount up front and a percentage of the remainder to the owner each month. If you can assume a low mortgage interest rate, even with the extra payment to the owner each month, your total payment could be significantly lower than a new mortgage. Therefore, the property may be easier to rent, because you could charge less than competitors.

BUYING A SECOND HOUSE OR CONDO

From your perspective, one of the nicest scenarios occurs when the seller owns the house outright and can act as the lender. In this case, the interest rate of the loan could be very low, particularly if the seller is interested in a long-term monthly income rather than cash for his house. Even though the interest rate he receives may be lower than that of a conventional bank mortgage, it could still be higher than he could find in other investments.

Several factors to consider before buying a rental property are rentability, neighborhood, affordability, and a minimum down payment. Hiring a professional inspector before buying is important to make sure the property's plumbing, electrical system, and construction are in good condition.

INVESTMENT RECAP

Type of investment. Buying a second condominium or house.

Time frame of investment. Long-term; probably the length of a mortgage.

Risk/reward level. Although most people believe real estate to be a fairly safe investment, this particular recommendation is rated fairly risky at a 6–7. This is because of the many variables to consider. These include price, location, down payment, financing, taxes, and rentability. Despite the risks, the rewards can be significant. A small down payment could eventually blossom into a fully owned piece of rental property.

Level of attention needed. All real estate needs attention, and this is no exception. Making sure that the property is maintained (either by yourself or by a management company) is important to maintain the quality of your investment. Making sure the rent is paid and that the tenants are not devaluating your investment is important.

Amount of expertise needed. When it comes to creative financing, hiring a good real estate attorney is essential. This investment also needs a lot of research to make sure that your property has potential for an increase in value.

Caveats and pitfalls. It is a complicated investment. There are many things to consider and if one goes seriously wrong, your principal investment could be endangered. Be prepared to give this investment the attention it needs and deserves. If you cannot do that, you will probably be better off with one of the other types of investments recommended in this publication.

Savings Passbook Alternatives

RISK LEVEL: 1–2

Once-simple bank savings and checking accounts have taken on whole new structures within the last few years, some of which are unfamiliar to the average investor. Given current low interest rates, the 5½ percent offered on passbook savings accounts is not a poor return now, but throughout most of the last fifteen years, it has been so-so to terrible, depending on the rate of inflation and the level of market interest rates.

In the 1930s, the banks themselves, in cooperation with the federal government, wanted a ceiling on interest paid on savings accounts. Banks believed that if they did not have to compete with each other in order to lure savings deposits, they would not have to make "risky" investments. Confidence had to be restored to the banking system, and banks wanted to limit competition. Considering the precarious state of U.S. banking, it was about all they could do to guarantee their survival.

These low-paying, interest-bearing passbook savings and time deposit accounts (CDs) served the banking community very well. They made money and for years, customers stayed even with or slightly ahead of inflation. It was during the 1960s, when inflation started creeping up, that people began to notice that the yield of 5 percent-plus was not enough to make up for 4 percent annual inflation plus the taxes on the interest.

By the end of the 1970s, the banks were in deep trouble. Their own legislation was hurting their profits. New, nonbank money market mutual funds that invested in the safest paper in the world (United States Treasury bills) were enticing investors with their high market interest rates.

Money was flying out of passbook accounts into money market funds. At one point in late 1979 and early 1980, traditional savings passbooks were still paying 5½ percent and money market mutual funds were paying double-digit interest rates.

Banks began to realize that if they were to survive, they had to compete. Savings, market, and time deposits were no longer in the exclusive domain of the banking industry. Regulation Q, passed in the 1930s, which allowed the Federal Reserve to regulate the interest paid on various accounts by banks, was virtually dismantled.

On April 1, 1986, the cap of 5½ percent paid on regular savings passbooks came off. Now, since nobody has seen banks aggressively advertising much higher rates for these accounts, we can reasonably assume they will remain there, or creep up at a snail's pace. There are, however, two reasons why the interest rate paid on regular passbook savings has not been aggressively increased. First, market rates are low and so is inflation. Second, because of deregulation, banks offer alternatives to savings passbooks that pay higher rates of interest.

There is a trade-off, however. Passbooks offer low interest but are very flexible. You can take money out or deposit it in any denomination and virtually at will during normal banking hours. Many banks require a minimum balance of only $100 on a savings passbook account. The higher yields and the yields being offered on accounts that traditionally paid no interest have less flexibility than passbook accounts in general, or some kind of minimum balance requirement that is substantial. The new accounts also have something that nonbank money market mutual funds don't have — insurance up to $100,000 on accounts in member banks of the Federal Deposit Insurance

Corporation (FDIC). Although the amount of money in FDIC coffers would save but a small percentage of the entire banking system, it's somehow seen as a psychological advantage over the noninsured money market mutual fund.

RECOMMENDED SAVINGS PASSBOOK ALTERNATIVES

New or relatively new alternatives to traditional passbook accounts include NOW and SUPER-NOW checking, money market deposit accounts (MMDA), and Jumbo CDs.

Here is how the end of Regulation Q stacks up for these various accounts:

NOW checking. The interest rate on noncommercial accounts is regulated at 5¼ percent. After January 1, 1986, banks did not have to demand a balance minimum on NOW accounts. Banks do have the right to demand a minimum balance before interest is paid, or if penalties or service charges are to be avoided.

The advantage of a NOW checking account is that you earn passbook rates on your money.

SUPER-NOW checking. The SUPER-NOW is similar to the regular NOW except that the interest rate is not set at 5¼ percent. The banks have the right to offer any rate, including money market rates. The requirement that the account maintains a $1,000 minimum balance was also waived on January 1, 1986.

The banks control the service charges and minimum balance to avoid service charges, and the minimum balance to earn interest or avoid penalty. Lately, some banks have offered SUPER-NOW accounts with only a $500 minimum requirement.

Money market deposit accounts (MMDA). The MMDA is a step up from the SUPER-NOW in that the individual banks not only control the interest rates, they also usually offer higher rates. MMDAs have no regulation that a minimum balance be required after January 1, 1986. The trade-off against the SUPER-NOW is that the number of pre-authorized withdrawals are limited to six per month and the minimum check-writing amount per check is often several hundred dollars.

Time deposits, or CDs. These are much the same as before, with the familiar penalties for early withdrawal. Jumbo CDs (those with minimum investments of $100,000) are now available to groups of people with less than $100,000 to invest. The bank takes care of the paperwork and the accounts are still insured by the FDIC. Of course, there are severe financial penalties if you withdraw your funds before maturity. Perhaps the most valuable aspect to this investment is that Jumbo CDs often pay as much as 1 or 2 percent more than the regular CDs of the same maturity.

Two ways you can find out which banks are paying the highest rates and offer the most services are:

Consult the *Savers Rate News,* P.O. Box 143520, Coral Gables, FL 33114 ($49.00 per year).

Bank Rate Monitor, P.O. Box 402608, Miami Beach, FL 33140 ($395.00 per year).

These publications are carried by many libraries, so you don't have to buy them.

If you don't need all your money liquid, there are some excellent advantages to using some of these new passbook alternatives. For example, instead of putting $1,000 each year in a passbook, let's assume you put that $1,000 yearly deposit into an MMDA that is tied to T bill rates. With an MMDA, you can get to the money by writing a check. Let's assume you never need any part of the savings. Over a period of, say, twenty-five years, it could make a tremendous difference in your retirement picture. The following table shows how each $1,000 yearly deposit would grow with only a 2 percent yield difference between the regular passbook and the MMDA. The example percent increase is compounded annually. Many MMDAs will be compounded daily.

SAVINGS PASSBOOK ALTERNATIVES

Year	5 percent	7 percent
1	$1,050	$1,060
2	$2,153	$2,215
3	$3,310	$3,440
4	$4,526	$4,751
5	$5,802	$6,153
10	$13,207	$14,784
15	$22,657	$26,888
20	$34,719	$43,865
25	$50,113	$67,676

The 2 percent increase adds up to a final monetary difference of $17,563. Imagine what could happen if you could get better than a 2 percent difference over long periods of time!

One of the best things about this investment is that it is not only insured by the FDIC, but you can conveniently find out about it in greater detail at your local banks. All banks have somebody that can easily explain their new alternatives to the traditional passbook savings account.

INVESTMENT RECAP

Type of investment. Savings passbook alternatives.

Time frame of investment. The new interest-bearing accounts being offered by banks in the wake of the abolishment of Regulation Q can be invested for a few months or many decades. Their flexibility is good.

Risk/reward level. At a rating of 1–2, passbook alternatives are the least risky of any investment in this book. They are very safe, being insured by the FDIC. Of course, market interest rates are better than the old, arbitrarily low rates of the past, but they are certainly not as good as the potential of some of the other investments listed in this book. For older people, using passbook alternatives may be a wise move for keeping their money secure *and* gaining a few more percentage points in return for their investment.

Level of attention needed. For the most part, very little attention is needed. Moving money from MMDAs into CDs may be important if rates go up quickly, but for the most part this is a relaxing form of investment.

Amount of expertise needed. You may want to "lock in" a very high rate. That would necessitate a change from one account to another.

Caveats and pitfalls. The only pitfall here is lost opportunity. If you move your money from, for example, a SUPER-NOW into a CD, and interest rates later move up substantially, you missed an opportunity. Also, you must be aware that you can't write checks frequently or in small amounts on some of the higher-paying accounts.

Glossary

AAA bonds:
The best-rated bonds. The interest payments on government AAA bonds are often insured, making them the most secure of all bonds.

After-tax return:
The return of an investment after taxes.

Allocation strategist:
The person who directs the relative monetary positions in the sub-funds of a large mutual fund.

Annuity:
A contract usually sold by an insurance company that provides for a fixed sum of money to be paid over a fixed period of time, or for life, in exchange for a sum of money.

CONSUMER GUIDE®

Appreciate:
To increase in value.

Artificial intelligence:
Machines with the ability to think and create
ideas.

Asset:
An item that has commercial value.

Assume a mortgage:
Taking over a seller's mortgage at the existing
interest rate.

Bear market:
A market that is generally trending down.

Blue chip:
In stocks, the best or high quality companies.

Bond:
A debt instrument. When a bond is purchased, a
loan is given to the issuing company or government in exchange for interest payments.

Bond fund:
A mutual fund which specializes in buying and
selling all kinds or selected types of bonds. Mutual
funds use the pooled money of investors to get
the best possible interest rates.

Bond rating:
An estimate made by an agency of the financial
strength of the bond issuer.

GLOSSARY

Broker:
A person who acts as an agent for a company that buys and sells securities or other investment products.

Bull market:
A market that is generally trending up in price.

Buy down:
When a seller of residential property pays the bank cash in return for lowering the monthly mortgage payments of a prospective buyer of the residential property.

CAD:
Computer-aided design.

Call:
A provision that allows a security to be redeemed at a specified time before its maturity.

CAM:
Computer-aided manufacturing.

Capital gain/loss:
The difference in value of a capital asset between when it was bought and sold.

Cash value:
The paid-for value of insurance.

Catalyst:
A chemical or element that speeds up a chemical reaction.

Caveat:
A warning. In investments, a particular problem that commonly arises.

CD:
Certificate of Deposit, a time deposit at a bank.

Common stock:
A unit of ownership in a corporation.

Compound interest:
Compound interest is interest that is added to an account on a regular basis throughout the year instead of just at the end of the year (simple interest). For example, a 7 percent compound interest will yield more than 7 percent interest on a given investment at the end of a year.

Consumer spending:
A statistic kept by the federal government that measures how much consumers spend each month. High consumer spending indicates growth in the economy.

Conversion ratio:
The number of common stock shares yielded by a convertible security.

Convertible bond:
A security that is issued like a bond, but can convert into a particular number of common stock shares in the company that issued the bond.

GLOSSARY

Corporate bonds:
Debt instruments issued by a corporation.

Coupon rate:
The rate of interest paid on a bond.

Cryogenics:
The science of super-cooling organic tissues so they can be stored and then revitalized at a later date.

Current yield:
Income received, divided by the current value or cost of the security.

Default:
When a person, government, or country refuses to pay an installment on a loan or a whole loan.

Deficit spending:
The amount of money a government spends beyond what it receives in taxes and other revenues.

Deflation:
A contraction of the volume of available money or credit that results in a decline of the general price level.

Depreciation:
Tax terminology reflecting a decrease in the value of an asset.

Discount security:
A security sold at a price below its face value.

Dividend:
A portion of money distributed to shareholders of a corporation as determined by a variety of factors.

Dow Jones averages:
Stock indicators published by Dow Jones & Co.; based on performance of a fixed portfolio.

Earned income:
Money earned through salary and/or wages, as opposed to money earned through investments.

Economic indicators:
A variety of measures of the economic health of business and industry as determined by the U.S. Department of Commerce.

Equity REIT:
A Real Estate Investment Trust that invests only in property.

Euroconvertibles:
Convertible securities offered in European markets.

Face value:
The principal amount of a security that will be paid at maturity.

GLOSSARY

FDIC:
Federal Deposit Insurance Corporation. It insures individual bank accounts up to $100,000 for member banks.

Federal Housing Administration (FHA):
A branch of government that guarantees certain mortgage loans, resulting in lower interest rates for borrowers.

Federal Reserve System:
The banking system of the federal government.

Federal Savings and Loan Insurance Corporation (FSLIC):
An agency sponsored by the U.S. government that guarantees individual cash assets up to $100,000 placed in member savings and loan associations.

General obligation bond:
A municipal security carrying the pledge of the issuer to repay the bond by using its full taxing authority.

GNP:
Gross national product. All the goods and services produced in a country in one year.

Government National Mortgage Association (GNMA):
A government agency that buys mortgages from lenders and issues mortgage pass-through certificates. These investments are commonly called Ginnie Maes.

Government securities:
Debt instruments issued by the U.S. government and its agencies.

Hedging:
The practice of protecting an investment position by using other markets.

Hybrid REIT:
A Real Estate Investment Trust that both invests directly in real estate and also participates in mortgages.

Hybrid security:
A convertible bond or stock.

Illiquid:
Generally referring to an investment that cannot be quickly converted to cash.

Indexing:
Use of a statistical measure of change in value, usually to apply some standard comparison or adjustment.

Inflation:
An increase in the volume of money, credit, and general price level. Typically measured by several key factors.

GLOSSARY

Inflation rate:
The monthly or annual rate of price increases.

Instrument:
A vehicle for investing money.

Interest:
The lender's fee charged a borrower for the use of his money.

Interest rate:
The cost of borrowing money.

IRA:
Individual Retirement Account.

Issue:
Securities or stock sold by a corporation or government.

Leverage:
The use of borrowed money involved in an investment.

Life annuity:
A contract that provides for lifetime payments of a fixed sum of money to be paid in exchange for a sum of money.

Liquidity:
The ease of selling an investment. High liquidity means that the investment is easy to sell.

CONSUMER GUIDE®

Load fund:
A mutual fund that charges a commission to individual investors for transactions. Usually, the commission is charged when buying *or* selling shares from a qualified plan.

Maturity:
The date on which the principal is due to a lender.

MMDA:
Money market deposit account.

Money market deposit account:
An account at a financial institution that pays interest rates on short-term deposits at the market rate.

Money market mutual fund:
A mutual fund that specializes in commercial and government paper, such as Treasury bills.

Mortgage REIT:
A Real Estate Investment Trust that invests exclusively in mortgages.

Municipal bonds:
Bonds issued by municipalities; usually the interest is exempt from federal income tax.

Mutual fund:
A professionally managed investment fund that typically specializes in some investment area, such as money markets or blue-chip stocks. Shares are sold to the public.

GLOSSARY

Negotiable security:
A security that can be sold or traded.

No-load fund:
A mutual fund that does not charge a commission to individual investors for transactions.

NOW:
A relatively new type of checking account that pays interest on deposits.

OPEC:
Organization of Petroleum Exporting Countries.

Option:
A financial product that allows a person to buy a specific commodity at a specific price during a specific period of time for a one-time payment called a premium.

Par:
The face value of a bond.

Passbook savings account:
A bank account that pays interest and is payable on demand.

Perpetual-life REIT:
A Real Estate Investment Trust that functions indefinitely into the future.

Platinum noble:
A coin made of platinum.

Precious metals:
Usually refers to gold, platinum, and silver.

Premium:
The amount of money you pay for insurance, either in a single payment or multiple yearly, quarterly, or monthly payments.

Price-earnings ratio:
The market price of a share divided by its annual earnings per share.

Prime rate:
The interest rate charged by banks to high quality, low-risk corporate borrowers.

Principal:
The amount of money invested.

Producer prices:
The prices asked by producers. An index kept by the government. Increasing producer prices indicate potential future inflation.

Purchasing power:
The value of a monetary unit in terms of the goods and services it can buy.

Real rate of return:
The return on an investment after accounting for taxes and inflation.

GLOSSARY

Recession:
A serious slowdown in the economy, usually indicated by three or more months of negative or no growth.

Regulation Q:
The 1930s law that regulated interest rates that could be paid on bank deposits. Now deregulated entirely.

REIT:
Real Estate Investment Trust.

Return:
The profit on an investment before taxes. This includes current income and growth or loss in the value of the assets. Sometimes called *total return*.

Risk/reward:
A term which applies to all investments. In general, the greater the risk, the greater the reward. Risk is the level of probability that the original investment will lose value. Reward is the level of potential earnings from the investment.

Savings bond:
A non-negotiable debt instrument issued by the U.S. Treasury at a discount from its face value.

Security:
A financial instrument that entitles the investor to specific rights, e.g., stocks and bonds.

Self-liquidating REIT:
A Real Estate Investment Trust that liquidates its assets at a predetermined time in the future.

Seller financing:
When the seller of a residential property monetarily helps the buyer of that property.

Share:
A unit of equity or ownership in a corporation or mutual fund.

Simple interest:
Interest that is paid on a savings account that is added to the account at the end of the year. For example, a 7 percent simple interest added to a $1,000 deposit at the end of the year makes the account worth $1,070.

Spread:
The difference between a bid and asked price on a security.

Stock mutual fund:
A mutual fund that specializes in buying and selling common stocks. They use pooled money from investors to diversify their portfolios or specialize in certain industries (e.g., high technology companies).

Stocks:
Shares issued by a company to raise money. The value of a stock often indicates the health and

profitability, or the trouble and financial problems, of a company.

Stop order:
An order to a broker or securities dealer to buy or sell at a price above or below market prices. A *stop-loss order* tells a broker to sell if prices drop to a certain level.

SUPER-NOW:
The latest in the NOW account checking deposits.

Tax bracket:
The percentage rate at which the last dollar of income earned is taxed.

Tax deferred:
The postponement of tax liability.

Tax-exempt bonds:
Bonds that are exempt from federal income taxes.

Tax-exempt security:
A debt instrument exempt from federal income tax.

Tax shelter:
A legal device that may avoid, lower, or defer income tax liability.

Third World debt:
The amount of money the undeveloped countries of the world owe the banks of the developed